Children of
DOMINICA

THE WORLD'S CHILDREN

Children of
DOMINICA

written and photographed by
FRANK STAUB

Carolrhoda Books, Inc./Minneapolis

For Barbara, Erin, and Molly

Text and photographs copyright © 1999 by Carolrhoda Books, Inc.
Photograph on page 6 (right) courtesy of the Library of Congress.
Map on page 9 by Bryan Liedahl © 1999 by Carolrhoda Books, Inc.

Carolrhoda Books, Inc., c/o The Lerner Publishing Group
241 First Avenue North, Minneapolis, MN 55401 U.S.A.

Website address: www.lernerbooks.com

LIBRARY OF CONGRESS CATALOGING-IN-PUBLICATION DATA

Staub, Frank J.
    Children of Dominica / Frank Staub.
        p.   cm. — (The world's children)
    Includes index.
    ISBN 1-57505-217-2
    1. Dominica—Social life and customs—Juvenile literature.
2. Children—Dominica—Social life and customs—Juvenile literature.
I. Title. II. Series: World's children (Minneapolis, Minn.)
F2051.S83 1999   97-27943
972.9841—dc21

Manufactured in the United States of America
1 2 3 4 5 6 – JR – 04 03 02 01 00 99

There is a story that when Christopher Columbus returned from his second voyage to the New World in 1493, the king and queen of Spain asked him to describe one of the islands he had seen. Instead of painting a picture with words, the explorer crumpled up a piece of paper. He said the paper's creases and folds were like the island's tall mountains and deep canyons.

Christopher Columbus and his crew were the first Europeans to see Dominica. Columbus brought many goods back from the New World with him to Spain.

Vieille Case, which lies on Dominica's northern coast, is one of many towns in the country with a French name.

The Carib Indians who lived on the island called their mountainous home Waitukubuli, which means "tall is her body." The Caribs had come from other islands in the Caribbean Sea and had taken the island from the native Arawak people around A.D. 1000. Columbus named the island Dominica, the Latin word for Sunday. He had first spotted the island's high peaks jutting above the Caribbean Sea on a Sunday.

The mountains of Dominica made traveling difficult for the explorer and his crew, and the Caribs made it clear the newcomers were not welcome. In addition, the Spaniards found no gold in Dominica's hills, so Spain had little interest in taking over the island. Over the next few centuries, Europeans from other countries began arriving and settling in Dominica.

Many of the streams in Dominica have beautiful waterfalls.

A mural in the town of Massacre shows how the town got its name. In 1674, British settlers killed, or massacred, a group of Carib Indians at this spot.

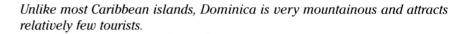
Unlike most Caribbean islands, Dominica is very mountainous and attracts relatively few tourists.

In the early 1700s, French and British settlers brought many African slaves to Dominica. They started planting crops and cutting the forests for lumber. For many years, France and Britain fought over the right to rule the island. Finally, in 1805, Britain gained full control. The British government freed the slaves in 1834 but held control of the island, called the Commonwealth of Dominica, until 1978. In that year, Britain gave Dominica its independence.

It's easy to confuse Dominica with the Dominican Republic because the names are similar. The Dominican Republic lies northwest of Dominica and shares the island of Hispaniola with Haiti. Hispaniola is part of a group of large Caribbean islands called the Greater Antilles. Dominica lies in the Lesser Antilles.

Like the other Lesser Antilles, Dominica is small—about 29 miles long and 16 miles wide. But unlike the other Antilles, both Greater and Lesser, Dominica hasn't changed much in 500 years. The deep canyons and steep mountains have kept people from settling much of the island. In addition, Dominica's rugged shoreline offers few sandy beaches, so Dominica has fewer tourists, hotels, and golf courses than most islands in the region. As a result, no other Caribbean island is blessed with so much of its original forest. Nor does any other look so much like it did when Columbus first arrived. That's why Dominica is often called the Nature Island of the Caribbean.

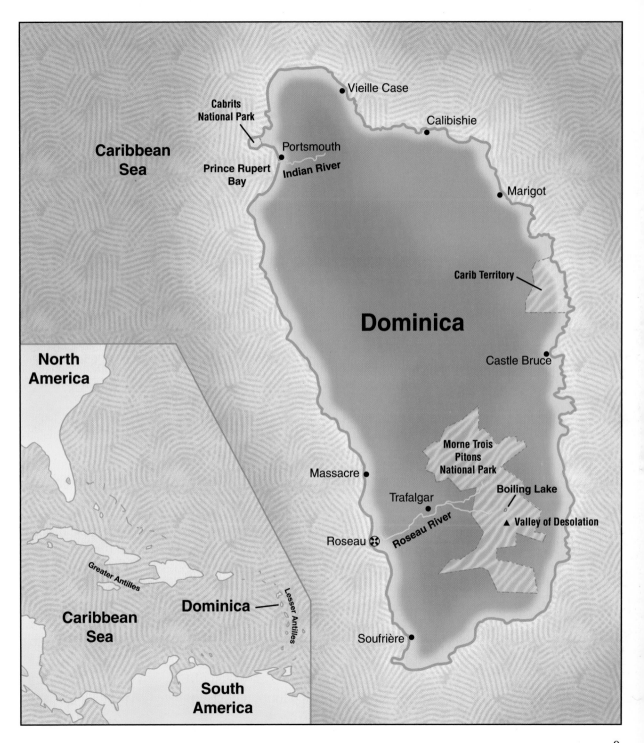

Mandi and Peter rest beside Boiling Lake. Like most Dominicans, they are descended from African slaves who were brought to Dominica by Europeans during the 1700s.

Although tourism is a small part of Dominica's economy, more and more foreign visitors come to Dominica each year. They come mainly to see the island's wild forests, beautiful birds, and other natural attractions. Mandi's father, Peter, works as a guide, taking tourists on hikes in the wilderness. Early in the morning, Peter and Mandi leave their home in Roseau, Dominica's capital city. They pick up a group of tourists and drive into the high country of Morne Trois Pitons National Park.

Then Mandi and the other hikers follow a trail up a steep slope. At the top, they enter a steaming land called the Valley of Desolation. Their goal is Boiling Lake, a scalding, bubbling pond in the mouth of an old volcano. The volcano is one of many that spewed out hot rocks and lava millions of years ago to form the island of Dominica. Some of the fiery material still lies below the island's surface. The hot rock heats underground water, which bubbles to the surface. In some places, underground water turns to steam and escapes through cracks in the earth. The rising steam gives the Valley of Desolation its mysterious appearance.

Peter leads tourists through the Valley of Desolation.

Soon after Mandi and the others leave Boiling Lake, rain begins to fall. Dominica is a very rainy place. The higher parts of the island receive more than 300 inches of rain each year. Because of all the rain, some say, the island has 365 rivers and streams. That makes one for each day of the year.

Despite the rain, the hikers don't get cold. Dominica's temperature hardly ever falls below 70 degrees Fahrenheit, even in the winter. A warm, wet climate like Dominica's is called a tropical climate. An amazing variety of plants grow in tropical areas, and Dominica is no exception. Rain forests cover over two-thirds of the island's land surface. More than 1,000 species of flowering plants are found on Dominica.

The rain forests of Dominica provide homes for many kinds of plants and animals, such as the Jaco parrot (left) and the anolis tree lizard (below).

Dominica's lush forests provide food and shelter for all kinds of wild animals. More than 160 species of birds live on the island. One of Mandi's favorite birds is the Jaco parrot. She knows a lot about the plants and animals of the forest. Sometimes she thinks she might like to be a guide herself someday, just like her father.

Roseau, Dominica's capital and largest city, lies on the southwestern coast.

Dominicans rarely worry about the weather, except during hurricane season. Hurricanes are violent storms that usually occur in late summer and early fall. During a hurricane, winds can reach 150 miles per hour, stirring up the sea and blowing down trees and buildings.

Although Peter likes to laugh and tell jokes, he gets very serious when he talks about hurricanes. In 1979, a dangerous storm known as Hurricane David struck Dominica. It wrecked Peter's house and injured some of his friends. The hurricane damaged many buildings and crops, and it killed more than 50 people.

Hurricanes are especially scary in Dominica because almost everyone on the island lives along the coast. These big storms can send huge waves crashing into coastal cities and towns.

Randy, Lloyd, Trisha, and Shadina don't worry about hurricane waves because they live high on the side of a mountain in the town of Trafalgar, near the trail to Boiling Lake. But they receive even more rain throughout the year than do people living in the lowlands along the coast.

Left: *Randy, Lloyd, Trisha, and Shadina in Trafalgar.* Above: *This school bus was crushed during Hurricane David in 1979 and has never been removed from the spot.*

15

Of Dominica's 75,000 residents, about 15,000 live in the capital city of Roseau. Roseau is a big city for such a small island. But very few buildings are more than two stories high. Most homes in Roseau are made of wood or concrete. In general, they have few rooms and little furniture. Most Dominicans cannot afford large, modern homes.

Carmen lives in an older home in Roseau. Every day, she sweeps her front yard with a broom made from the leaves of a coconut tree. Coconut trees grow everywhere on the island. Their leaves and fruit have many uses. Carmen's mother made the broom by cutting coconut leaves into strips and tying them together.

After she finishes sweeping, Carmen will help clean the house.

Roseau at sunset

Down at the beach, Carmen's friend Ian plays on a swing made from a coconut tree branch. Like most Dominicans, Carmen and Ian speak two languages: English, the country's official language, and French Creole. This language contains many French words, as well as words from African languages brought to Dominica by African slaves. Some Creole words come from the Carib Indian language. People on other Caribbean islands, such as Guadeloupe, Martinique, and Haiti, speak similar forms of French Creole.

Left: *Ian swings on a coconut tree by the sea.* Above: *A typical Roseau street*

Students in Roseau return from school, while a cruise ship docks in the harbor.

Most of Dominica's important business takes place in Roseau. The city is also Dominica's main port. Large ships carrying products to and from Dominica dock there. In 1979 Hurricane David destroyed Roseau's main pier, or docking area. Many years passed be- fore a new pier could be built.

The name Roseau comes from the French word *roseau,* meaning reed, a type of plant. Reeds grow along the Roseau River nearby. For Garvey, the Roseau River is a good place to give Ned the horse a bath. Garvey takes care of Ned for the horse's owner. The owner lives farther inland, where there isn't as much grass for Ned to eat. Garvey brings Ned to the river, where there's lots of grass. In return, Garvey gets to ride Ned whenever he wants to.

Across the river, Kyle catches fish for a school science experiment about the dangers of alcohol. He wants to put some fish in a jar of water and others in a jar that also contains rum, an alcoholic drink made from sugarcane grown nearby. Then he wants to measure how long it takes the fish in the rum to die.

Kyle catches fish in the Roseau River, while Garvey washes Ned.

Ian drinks from a faucet after school. He will come back later with a bucket to get water for his family.

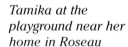

Tamika at the playground near her home in Roseau

In another part of Roseau, Tamika spends her afternoon at the grafitti-covered playground near her home. So far, she hasn't had to worry about crime, drugs, and other big-city problems as much as children in many parts of the world do. Making enough money to survive is the biggest concern of most Dominican families.

Most people in Dominica do not have much money. They live off the land as much as they can. Electrical appliances and other kinds of technology are expensive because they must be shipped from other countries.

Even in Roseau, many houses do not have running water. Ian and his family get their water from faucets by the road. Some Dominicans have modern gas stoves, but most people cook with wood-burning stoves. Hilroy and Vincent live in Vieille Case, on the northern coast of the island. They carry loads of firewood home to their mother. To cut the firewood, the boys use long knives they call cutlasses.

Farm animals are a luxury in Dominica because they are expensive to buy and to feed. Leanna and her family are lucky. In the small town of Calibishie, they raise goats for meat and milk. Most Dominican families usually cannot afford to buy these food items.

Leanna, her father, and other family members feed their goats.

About once a week, Hilroy and Vincent cut firewood for their mother.

Niver likes coming to the Roseau market with her father. After they finish selling fruits and vegetables, they go shopping.

Most Dominicans make at least part of their living from farming, or agriculture. Niver and her father, Edison, sell fruits and vegetables at Roseau's open-air market. During the week, Edison works as a mason, laying bricks for houses and walls. But every Saturday, Edison and Niver come to Roseau to sell things the family has grown in their yard. Dominica's rainy climate and rich volcanic soil make it easy to grow all sorts of crops.

Even for people who don't grow food on their own, the Roseau market holds opportunities for making a living. Near Niver and Edison's spot, Eric sells ginger and a kind of squash called pumpkin. Eric's pumpkins are different from the pumpkins Americans use to make pies and jack-o'-lanterns. Eric and his family bought the pumpkins from a farmer. They sell them at the market for a higher price.

Eric lives many miles from Roseau. Since the market opens soon after sunrise, Eric has to get up at 3:00 A.M. to catch a bus to get there on time.

Part of Roseau's market is indoors. Here Seraphine and her son David cook chicken pilau, one of Dominica's most popular dishes. It is made with chicken, rice, and spices.

Dominicans do much of their food shopping at markets like the one in Roseau. They also shop at grocery stores, especially for canned goods and cleaning prod-

ucts. In Calibishie, Ulica works at her family's store. She says that many items they sell are expensive because they must order them from other countries.

In Marigot, people gather around a fishing boat to buy dinner, while Michel cleans fish.

Because so many Dominicans live along the coast, fish is common dinner fare. In Marigot, on Dominica's eastern coast, a boat returns from a fishing trip. People gather around to buy their dinner. Michel works for one of the fishers, cleaning fish for the customers.

In Dominica, dolphinfish, tuna, snapper, cavali, bonito, kingfish, jack, flying fish, and balaou are all in demand. But so many fish have been caught in Dominica's waters that it's getting harder for fishers to find fish. So most fishers have a second job, usually working on a farm.

Phaedra's family lives up the road from the Marigot fishing dock. They grow bananas, Dominica's main product to sell to other countries. But Dominica competes with many other tropical countries that also export bananas. That is one reason Dominica is such a poor nation. Phaedra's family also grows vegetables for their own use. But sometimes they can get only old vegetable seeds, which don't grow very well.

Brian and Rosmund

Near Phaedra's home, Brian and his cousin Rosmund walk to school. They bring along orange juice to have with their lunch. Oranges and other citrus fruits such as grapefruit and lemons are important crops in Dominica. Making juice from those fruits is one of Dominica's few industries.

Phaedra leans on a banana tree near her home in Marigot.

This cannon still seems to stand guard at Fort Shirley.

Throughout Dominica's history, ships from many nations have arrived in Prince Rupert Bay on the island's northwestern coast. The bay was once a popular stop for pirates. Ships are protected there from ocean storms and big waves, so pirate ships could hide there safely.

During the years when they struggled over control of Dominica, French and British sailors stopped in the bay for fresh water, fruit, and firewood. Later, the British built the city of Portsmouth next to Prince Rupert Bay. Since then, Portsmouth has grown into the second-largest city in Dominica. Fishing boats, sailing yachts, and cruise ships now anchor in the busy harbor.

Ray and his friends live in Portsmouth. Sometimes they visit Cabrits National Park, located on the northern shore of Prince Rupert Bay. The park's main attraction is Fort Shirley. The British began building the fort in 1770 to protect the harbor from the French. They fired cannonballs at any French ships that came near. From 1778 to 1783, the French took over Dominica and used the fort to fire on the British. Some of Fort Shirley's crumbling walls still stand, and some of the original cannons are still there.

From Fort Shirley, Ray (left) and his friends *can look out over Prince Rupert Bay and the city of Portsmouth.*

Diamond shares a home in Portsmouth with his father, Roger. Diamond likes to play with his toys in their small front yard. Roger works as a boatman, taking tourists for rowboat rides on the Indian River south of town. Many men in Portsmouth make their living in this way.

On many days, there are not enough tourists to keep all the boatmen working. For Roger, today was one of those days. He didn't find anyone to take for a ride, so he didn't make any money. Diamond and Roger will not be able to buy food for dinner tonight. They will make do with rice from the night before.

Diamond and his father live in a house built on stilts. This will help keep it dry if a hurricane ever sends ocean waves into Portsmouth.

Randolph, another tour guide, has better luck. A customer hires him for a boat ride. Randolph's daughter Fedorra rides along. The river winds through dark, tropical forests and banks covered with the big roots of mang trees. While the visitor explores the forest, Randolph bails out water that has leaked into the boat, and Fedorra looks for birds flying among the trees.

Fedorra and Randolph. The red, yellow, and green colors on Randolph's boat and hat symbolize his African ancestry.

A Dominican guide rows a boat full of tourists down the Indian River.

After the boat ride, Randolph and Fedorra go home to Fedorra's mother, Claudia, and two sisters, Anorra and Midorra. After a dinner of chicken pilau, Fedorra and Anorra dance to the radio while Midorra washes dishes.

Later, the girls watch television. The only television station they get in Portsmouth is broadcast from the nearby island of Guadeloupe. The television programs are in French. The girls understand a few French words, which are similar to the French Creole they speak at home.

Randolph and his family at the front door of their home

Midorra washes dishes outside with water she carried from a public faucet.

Fedorra and Anorra dance in their bedroom. Pictures cut out of magazines decorate their walls.

Fedorra and her family are lucky to own a radio and a television. Like most Dominicans, they have little money. On many days, Randoph cannot find any work. Their house has only two small rooms. Randolph and Claudia sleep in one room. The girls sleep in the other on a piece of foam rubber they bring out at night.

Midorra and Anorra go to the Portsmouth Government School. Dominican children are required to attend primary school between the ages of 5 and 12. If students pass a special test, they can go on to secondary school, which lasts up to age 17.

From the 1800s until the 1960s, schools in Dominica were run by Catholic and Methodist churches. Nearly all primary schools are now run by the government. Half of Dominica's secondary schools are run by churches and half by the government.

Anorra (far right) *with her friends at school*

Dominica also has a small number of preschools, for which parents usually pay a small fee.

The children in Merlyn Hunter's fifth-grade class learn math, spelling, grammar, history, and science. Like other Dominican students, they wear uniforms to school.

Merlyn Hunter teaches a fifth-grade class at the Portsmouth Government School.

Children between the ages of two and five attend the Crayfish River Preschool.

The Carib Territory looks much like the rest of the Dominican countryside.

After Europeans began colonizing the Caribbean islands, Carib Indians from many of the islands moved to Dominica. They came to hide from the Europeans among the steep, rugged mountains and valleys. In Dominica, the Caribs fought fiercely to keep the intruders away.

For 200 years after Columbus's arrival, no European country was able to conquer Dominica. Even after the French claimed the island in 1627, the Caribs continued to resist their rule. But the long years of fighting took their toll on the Carib population. By 1730, only 400 Caribs remained. Today, about 2,000 Caribs live in Dominica. They live mostly in an area on the central eastern coast known as the Carib Territory. This land was set aside by the British in 1902 for the sole use of the Carib people. Dominica is the only island in the Caribbean that has land reserved for Caribs.

Over the years, many Caribs married descendants of African slaves. Agenette and Bruce are two of many Dominicans who have both Carib and African ancestors. They have curlier hair and rounder faces than their Carib ancestors. Still, they live in the Carib Territory and consider themselves to be Caribs.

This woman works on a banana farm in the Carib Territory.

Agenette and Bruce eat papaw for breakfast. Their mother sells papaw and other fruits at a nearby roadside stand.

For centuries, the Carib Indians have been known for their skill at making dugout canoes. Manuel has been making canoes since he was a young man. He carves his canoes out of a single log, just like his ancestors did. They used these boats for fishing, which has been an important part of Carib culture and survival.

The Carib Territory is perched high above the water on steep cliffs. It has few places from which people can launch boats. Instead of being fishers, most Caribs are now farmers. They grow bananas, coconuts, and other fruits and vegetables. But rather than selling their crops, Caribs in the territory share most of the foods they grow with each other. They treat their land as if it were a big family farm.

With help from some friends, Manuel (holding hammer) builds a dugout canoe that is much like the canoes used by his ancestors.

In the Carib Territory, there are few places where boats can enter and leave the sea safely.
Inset: Like most Dominicans, this Carib corn farmer depends on the land for survival.

In general, Caribs have even less money for toys and other things than most Dominicans have. So Carib children make good use of the plants that grow all around them. Juliet has turned some coconut leaves into a toy windmill. Vernillia and Chertly know that a bunch of flowers makes a great gift for their teacher.

Kervel attends the Sinelo Primary School in the Carib Territory. She and her classmates help take care of the land around their school. Plants grow quickly in Dominica's tropical climate, and weeds in the schoolyard can become very thick. Kervel and her friends sometimes clear out the weeds by cutting them down.

Vernillia and Chertly with flowers for their teacher

Juliet made these windmills with leaves from a coconut tree like the ones behind her.

Amandine and Kervel weave baskets out of leaves. They use designs that have been passed down for many generations.

After school, Kervel and her cousin Amandine use long, thin leaves to make traditional Carib baskets. The girls' parents buy the leaves while they are still green and cut them into strips. After a week or two, the leaves become dry and brown. Then the girls soak some of the leaves in mud until they turn a rich black color. To make white leaves, they peel off the undersides of the leaves. It takes about a day for one of the girls to weave a large basket. A small basket takes half a day. Kervel and Amandine learned how to weave from their mothers.

At the Salybia Government School in the Carib Territory, classrooms are often too small for all the students. So Sherril, Natherlice, and Hyacinthe must do the homework for their food and nutrition class on the porch.

A physical education class at the school could use more space too. Balls that are hit too far go into the sea. The children often play rounders, a British game in which a batter hits a ball and runs around bases. A short bat is usually used in a rounders game. But the children don't have one, so they use a coconut tree branch instead.

Sherril, Natherlice, and Hyacinthe do homework on the porch of the Salybia Government School.

A physical education class plays rounders. The game of baseball developed partly from this British sport.

A cricket match in Castle Bruce

Beth and Davidson practice cricket using sticks and a coconut branch. Beth is the striker, and Davidson is the bowler.

Beth uses a coconut branch to hit a ball too. He and his friend Davidson are practicing cricket. Like rounders, cricket is a British game played by two teams. A player called the bowler throws the ball toward the batter, or striker, who tries to hit it. A wicket behind the striker has three stumps with two bails on top. The bowler tries to hit the wicket so that a bail falls off.

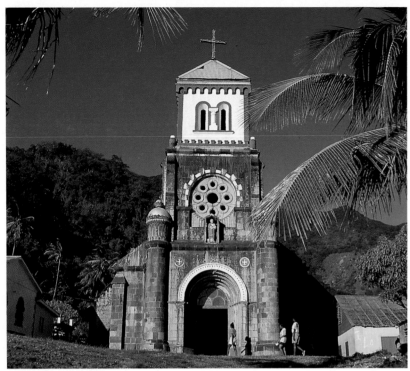

Saint Mark's Catholic Church in Soufrière. Most Dominican towns have at least one church, usually Catholic.

Nakita and Royette in costume at the Roseau Carnival celebration

French colonists brought the Catholic religion to Dominica in the 1700s. Most Dominicans—about 80 percent—are still Catholic. Most of the rest are Protestants.

Like nearly all Christians, Dominicans celebrate Christmas and Easter. But the favorite holiday of most Dominicans is Carnival. It occurs on the Monday and Tuesday before Ash Wednesday, in late winter or early spring.

Nakita lives in Roseau. She and her friends spend weeks getting ready for Carnival. Like hundreds of other Dominicans, the girls dress up in costumes and march in Roseau's big Carnival parade. This year, Nakita won the Miss Carnival Princess contest. Her friend Royette came in second.

Many Dominicans dress in modern costumes for the Carnival parade. But some wear clothing from Dominica's past. Many women and girls wear long dresses like those worn when the island was a French colony in the 1700s. Kemai represents Dominica's past too. He walks on stilts in the parade. Slaves from Africa brought the activity of walking on stilts to Dominica. It took Kemai only a few days to learn how to do it.

Stilts keep Kemai (wearing red pants) three feet off the ground. For next year's parade, he hopes to use four-foot stilts.

Carnival parade participants in French colonial dress

The best part of Carnival for Adler and Nadine is the "jump-up" after the parade. During jump-up, two trucks drive slowly around town. Each truck has a popular band and lots of big speakers. As the bands play, Adler, Nadine, and hundreds of other Dominicans crowd around the trucks and jump up—they do a marchlike dance in time to the music.

Music fills the air during Carnival, as people bring out their instruments and play. Much of Dominica's music is similar to that of other Caribbean islands, where calypso music is very popular. But Dominica's music has many differences because it has been influenced by four different cultures: French, British, African, and Carib. Rhythm is a big part of Dominican music, so drums are especially important.

As the sun gets low on the last day of Carnival, Iachar marches up the street with other drummers. Iachar also plays in his high school band. The music and dancing will continue into the night.

Surrounded by people in parade costumes, Adler and Nadine jump up at Carnival.

Iachar plays his drum at Carnival.

Once again, Carnival has been a fun time. It has also been a time for Dominicans to take pride in their island nation. They recall their national motto, "Après Bondie C'est La Ter," which means "After God, It Is the Land" in French Creole. The motto refers to Dominica's dependence on agriculture. But for many, it also refers to their pride in the beautiful and unspoiled land of the country they call home.

Dominicans treasure the beauty of their land and sea.

More about Dominica

What is Dominica's relationship with Great Britain?

Dominica is a member of the Commonwealth of Nations. This is an association of about 50 independent nations throughout the world that were once under British rule and now cooperate with each other in foreign policy.

What kind of government does Dominica have?

Dominica is a democracy, with a prime minister and a legislature made up of 21 members who are chosen by the people and 9 members who are chosen by the government.

What kind of money do Dominicans use?

The Eastern Caribbean dollar. One Eastern Caribbean dollar, or EC, is worth about two and a half U.S. dollars. Antigua, Grenada, and half a dozen other islands in the Lesser Antilles use this currency.

Pronunciation Guide

Antilles an-TIH-leez
Cabrits kuh-BRITS
Calibishie ka-lih-BIH-shee
calypso kuh-LIP-soh
Carib KAR-ib
Caribbean Sea kehr-uh-BEE-uhn SEE
Dominica dah-muh-NEE-kuh
French Creole FRENCH KREE-ohl
Guadeloupe GWAH-duh-loop
Marigot mah-ree-GOH
Morne Trois Pitons MORN TRWAH
  pee-TOHN
Portsmouth PORT-smuhth
Roseau roh-ZOH
Trafalgar truh-FAL-guhr
Vieille Case vee-AY CASE
Waitukubuli why-too-koo-BOO-lee

Index